A Fat

A Collection of Published Short Stories

For Sandy, Savannah and Justin

The Stories

A Father's Heart

When I was a young man, there were two absolute, unchangeable truths in my life. I was going to be a rock and roll star, and I was never, ever going to have any children.

You've heard the one about making God laugh by telling him your plans?

Well, He must've had some gut-busters at my expense because I have long ago passed the place in my life where anyone should even think of selling me a pair of leather pants, and I have now fathered one-third of a baseball team.

A rock star? Nope.

A father? Got me good there, didn't ya, God?

Sandy, my oldest daughter, was born on July 21, 1988 in Williamsburg, Virginia. Savannah, my little girl, was born on August 24, 1996 in Hillerød, Denmark. About 12 years after Sandy and four years after Savannah, and long after I presumed I was finished doing my part to populate the planet, God chuckled one more time and my son Justin came along.

Each one of my kids is special and magical in their own way, and as different as they could possibly be and still be considered part of the same genome. I hope some of that will show up in the stories that follow.

One reason I wanted to scribble this little bunch of stories was to stick up for dads.

The media these days delights in presenting fathers as bumbling stooges blessed with zero parenting skills and devoid of even basic social graces. Every week it seems like there is yet another stupid Dad show on TV. Even a brilliant book like 'Angela's Ashes' looks at only the darkest side of fatherhood.

All dads are not idiots or drunken losers. In fact, I would submit that most of them aren't.

Full disclosure time.

I am divorced. My children have different mothers. Dawn is Sandy's mother, and Lotte is Savannah and Justin's mother. They are both wonderful women and moms, and, with occasional help from me, they are raising amazing children.

Finances and circumstances prevent me from spending as much time with Sandy as I would like to…or should. Being on the road prevents me from spending as much time with Savannah and Justin as I would like to…or should. The traveling and distances also places extra burdens on Dawn and Lotte and make me feel like a bad father.

Perhaps that is the real reason behind these little stories.

Chances are pretty good that I'll never be a rich man, so these pages may well be all I leave behind for my children. And won't they be pissed about that! But maybe, just maybe, they'll find something in here…

Some of these tales are well-worn and cherished memories. Others are happening faster than I can write them down. All of them are true. Well, at least as true as a Father's Heart remembers them. My sharing these thoughts doesn't mean that I am setting myself up as some sort of Dr. Phil-ish expert about fatherhood or anything else, because, Lord knows, I am not.

Me, I am just a father. And I love my kids. I think that still counts for something in the big ledger.

Anyway, I sure hope so.

So, here's the idea. The stories are here to read, and the links that pop up at the end of some of them are to songs that have a connection to the preceding tale. You can certainly read the stories without ever listening to the songs, and vice versa, but I always have music on in the background when I read, so why not music that actually has something to do with what you are reading? The first song, 'Confession', is pretty self-explanatory. A father trying to come to grips with himself and his failures...

All of the songs from A Father's Heart are available at http://weaverwrites. com/songs_from_a_fathers_heart

Confession

I'm not really proud, of everything I've done,
to shake myself free when I got the urge to run.
Left some hearts broken, left some debts unpaid,
when I heard that highway call, or some other sad cliche'

When they make whiskey a little stronger, highways a little longer,
I might really reach the place I feel no pain.
'Til then I ask forgiveness for things I cannot change,
and pity on a prisoner, bound by his own chains.

I've wasted a lifetime on passion's sweet lies,
'til I can't stand face-to-face with my own alibis.
Now the fiddler has his hand out, the piper stands unpaid,
and there's a child who bears the scars of each mistake I've made.

When they make whiskey a little stronger, highways a little longer,
I might really reach the place I feel no pain.
'Til then I ask forgiveness for things I cannot change,
and pity on a prisoner, bound by his own chains.

I'm not really proud, of everything I've done,
to shake myself free when I got the urge to run.

When they make whiskey a little stronger, highways a little longer,
I might really reach the place I feel no pain.
'Til then I ask forgiveness for things I cannot change,
and pity on a prisoner, bound by his own chains.

*All of the songs from A Father's Heart are available at http://weaverwrites.
com/songs_from_a_fathers_heart*

William R. Weaver, Sr.

Before I start rambling on about being a father, I should probably tell you a little bit about my own dad. It's always easier to get a bead on somebody if you know a little about where they come from. My dad, William R. Weaver, Sr., was not a particularly well-educated man. Like a lot of men of his generation he had to quit school at 14 and go to work. He was, however, a smart guy. He had a shed-load of common sense, and he knew how to fix what was broken and keep stuff going long after it should have been hauled off to the nearest junkyard.

Later on in life, I was amazed to find out that he liked to read. Beyond the Playboy that he always stashed in his bottom drawer (I just knew, OK?), I don't recall ever seeing him with a book or a magazine around the house. And yet, when he retired from General Motors, stashed in along with his uniforms and his tools there was a box full of paperbacks that he read during his breaks in the can.

My dad. Digging 'The Exorcist'. Who knew?

Dad liked good friends and loved a good joke, even a dirty one. He had no use for people that used foul language in front of women, but could turn the air a crackling blue when he was doing something around the house that wasn't working out to his satisfaction. The neighbors used to take their kids in the house when my dad was working outside.

Folks liked my dad and called him, as a compliment, "a regular guy".

Like Pap in Faulkner's 'Shingles for the Lord', my dad knew only one thing about work; when it wasn't done, it wasn't done, and when it was, it was. You used whatever means and tools you had to get the work done, and it was a man's job to turn a buck. No excuses, no bullshit, no matter what.

Along with his regular job, my dad cleaned wells, shingled roofs, hauled trash, fed hogs…whatever it took to earn a poor man's dollar. Legend has it that he was out catching chickens on the cold November night I was born. Dad drove mom to the hospital in his old truck with the heat blasting and the windows rolled up to keep her warm. He didn't realize how rank he was with the smell of what comes out of the back end of hen. And I don't mean eggs. He simply couldn't understand why the simple act of having a baby was making his pretty young wife so sick to her stomach.

During the carpentry years, when winter and the snow came and there was no work swinging a hammer, he went door-to-door like an 8-year-old kid asking to shovel sidewalks.

Now, my dad could rip it up with the best of them in his younger days. He apparently settled down right quick (with the help of the occasional well-placed shot to the head from mom) when us kids started showing up. But, like many new fathers, he didn't give up without a fight.

A well-loved family fable holds that when my sisters and I were still nearly babes and dad was still doing carpentry he would stop by Mollie's Tavern, a local watering hole, pretty much every day for "lunch". One day, we drove by Mollie's while we were all, including dad, out for a ride with Mom's well-off and snooty sister. I pointed at the old roadhouse, and just as cute as a three-year-old button, squeaked,

"That's where my daddy works."

Hey, that was where we picked him up most nights! I think if a hole had opened up in the earth, dad would have gladly crawled into it…and pulled me down with him.

Dad's days as a rounder were numbered once he married my mom. Nellie Weaver never took any crap off of anyone, including and especially her own husband. One Friday night when she decided that dad's 'lunch break' had gone on quite long enough, thankyouverymuch, she dressed herself to the nines, grabbed us kids, and we all hiked the half mile or so up to Mollies.

She plopped us down at a table, got us some Cokes and chips, and said,

"Weaver. Guess what…it's your night to baby-sit."

Now, my dad liked his beer and smoky, dim taverns, but his kids were by Christ NOT going to be seen sitting in a bar. As I recall, we got home in time to catch Cronkite. I didn't even get to finish my Coke.

My mom always put these things she called throw rugs on the floor. Just some little rugs to cover the door jams and the linoleum in front of the kitchen and bathroom sink.

Dad hated them with a passion, and was forever kicking and cussing them out. One night after a few 'short ones' with his buddies, he walked home from the local, and tripped on the throw rug in the kitchen…like he always did. So he started cussing it and kicking it… like he always did.

It didn't move. Not an inch. No matter how hard he kicked at it, it never budged.

He had only had a few, so he wasn't three-sheets-to-the-wind, but one sheet was definitely blowin' when dad got down on all fours and examined the rug, only to discover that mom had taken carpet tacks and nailed it to the floor.

He puttied the holes the next day and never said much about the throw rugs again.

Then there was the New Year's Eve when I was roped into looking after my sisters while the 'rents went out. My cousin Kenny and I had a mini-New Year's party of our own. Cokes, chips, a sip or two of a purloined PBR while watching Dick Clark drop that dumb-assed ball. We crashed at about one.

My folks came in at 6 a.m. I know this because my dad starting playing the piano and singing,

"It's six o'clock in the mornin', it's six o'clock in the mornin', oh, it's SIX O'CLOCK IN THE MORNIN', wake up, wake up, wake up…"

I think he wrote that song himself. And people wonder where I get my talent from.

Dad was not at all concerned that he could neither sing nor play the piano or that his captive audience was imparting that information to him with sleepy, raised voices. It is little wonder that my mother has never had a drink in her life.

Ray Weaver, Senior liked blue crabs, bluegrass and Blue Ribbon beer. He passed the appreciation of those pleasures on to his son. He sowed some wild oats in his younger days, but once his kids came along, he kept his nights out down to the occasional short beer after work, and a maybe a couple more on the weekends while he listened to some local band.

I was the singer in many of those bands. A lot of musicians talk about the troubles they had with their folks when they chose music as a career. Me, I will never have a bigger fan than my old man. From the Beatles and Stones and Creedence days, through the Grand Funk and Deep Purple haze, into my Dylan and Donovan phase and finally back home to Hank and Merle and the music he raised me on, he was there almost every weekend I played in town.

Ok he took a little break around the Marc Bolan/David Bowie period. I'm thinking the silver glitter platform shoes and purple eye-shadow may have put him off.

My dad will be the focus of a lot of the stories here, because anything that I am, I am because of him.

Somewhere in all of these words, I said that people called my dad a "regular guy."

To me, my dad was anything but regular.

He was my hero.

A Christmas Miracle, 1967

$14.99

That is what one Marx Vanity and Hassock for Little Girls cost at Christmastime in 1967. The vanity and hassock were molded out of white plastic, the vanity top lifted to reveal a genuine vinyl mirror and the drawer held a bunch of pink plastic lipsticks, makeup, and combs.

In 1967, the Marx Vanity was every little girl's dream.

My two middle sisters were 10 and 11 in 1967, and their eyes danced every time a commercial for the vanity lit up our ancient Motorola. They had both written to Santa asking for a vanity…and ripped the page out of the Sears Christmas catalogue and left it where my parents could find it…just in case the rumors they were hearing (mostly from their know-it-all 13-year-old brother) about Santa were true.

$14.99

Less than fifteen lousy bucks. But there were two girls, so that was almost 30 dollars.

Thirty dollars was simply more than my folks could go at Christmastime in 1967. They had 4 kids to buy for, and Christmas or no Christmas, there were still house payments and car payments and food to buy…the money just wasn't there.

My dad was a hardworking man, but there had been layoffs, and Christmas this year was going to be, well, slim.

I was a know-it-all 13-year-old in 1967, and I knew the score. Santa was broke.

My sisters were also pretty smart, so they didn't throw a fit when dad told them,

"Ol' Santa might not be able to bring the vanities this year, girls, but I am sure he'll have a nice doll or something."

They just bit their bottom lips and said, "OK, daddy."

I could hear them crying in their bedroom from my room across the hall. I know Dad heard them, too.

Our basement and attic were always off limits to kids during the Christmas season, and Christmas 1967 was no different. Santa and I had pretty much parted ways some years before (I say "pretty much" because I'm still sorta hedging that bet…no sense in taking chances) so I knew that the basement was my parent's staging area for whatever presents we would be getting.

Dad was always bringing scrap lumber home from work to burn in the wood stove, so I didn't think twice when he had me help him unload a bunch of oily, wooden machine parts boxes out of his truck and stack them by the backdoor. I figured we'd be splitting them into kindling in a few days.

Money or no money, Christmas was coming. Like every year before it signaled its approach with locked basements, tangerines, wood smoke and big ol', dangerously frayed, constantly shorting-out strings of multi-colored lights hung on the outside of the house.

There were no decorations inside yet, but that was normal. Santa not only brought our tree on Christmas Eve, he did our entire holiday interior decorating.

The inside of our house went from zero to a redneck Winter Wonderland in one magical, amazing night. I'm talking everything from a complete Lionel Train Garden to canned snow on the windows.

I had good, kid-friendly parents.

Something was indeed out of whack in our house, though.

My dad was a creature of habit. He was up early to work and home in time for dinner. He'd help us with our homework at the kitchen table, watch Cronkite and maybe 'Ironsides', then go to bed.

Day in, day out.

During December of 1967, though, he would help us with our homework and disappear straight into the basement where children's feet were forbidden to tread.

It was...weird.

Christmas Eve, 1967 came like it always does, and if my sisters were still dreaming of the Marx Vanity and Hassock for Little Girls, they didn't let on. We kids all went to bed early, like we always did, and then struggled to fall asleep, like we always did. We made about thirty trips - each - to the bathroom, to try and sneak a peek at what our parents were up to that was making so much noise.

My sisters worried that if my parents didn't quiet down soon, Santa would never show up at our house.

But show up he did...

They weren't plastic. They were wooden. They were hand-painted white and each vanity came with its own small hassock covered with a piece of red velveteen that looked suspiciously to me like some old drapes my mom had taken down the previous fall. Each vanity had its own small, standup mirror, and had not one, but two drawers filled with little girl's pretend makeup.

We had an aunt that worked at Kresge's, so I'm guessing she got Santa a discount on toy makeup.

My dad said, "Now, I know they don't look exactly like the ones on TV, but ol' Santa was hoping that you'd like these that he made himself in his workshop just as much."

They did.

Not too long ago, I found one of those old, wooden Christmas, 1967 vanities in my mother's basement. Dusty, stained, barely white anymore…but still standing and doing duty as a sewing table.

I wonder how many of those plastic ones are still around?

Requiem for the Maytag Man

Most of the men in my family are hunters and fishermen. The hunting thing never really took with me, though. Oh, I shot a few squirrels and rabbits growing up along Mountain Road - back when you could still hunt there. If you tried to hunt now in the same places we did back in the day you'd like as not wing a Taco Bell or a bag a grocery cart. I understand that there are, sadly, laws against that sort of thing.

It is hard for anyone stuck every morning and afternoon in endless rush hour traffic along what used to be a backwood country road to imagine how quiet it was around here just a few short decades ago.

There were no housing developments or fast food joints. There were no "cul-de-sacs". If I had heard the phrase "cul-de-sac" when I was a kid, I would have guessed that it was some sort of rash requiring calamine lotion.

Calamine lotion was big in our house. Every scrape, cut or insect bite I received, would wind up pink, crusty and smelly if I showed it to my mom. I am pretty sure that if one of the alligators that legend held lived in the swamps near the Chesapeake ever chomped off one of my limbs, my mom would have staunched the bleeding with a dish towel, made me a cup of tea and slathered the gushing stump with calamine lotion.

As far as I know, calamine lotion has never stopped anything or anybody from itching or hurting. You just wind up with pink crap under your finger nails from scratching anyway.

Anyway, as always, I digress…back to the hunt…

We ate what we shot in those days. My kids can't get behind the idea that I have actually eaten squirrel…and I liked it! We were regular Bubba Gump's of squirrel eaters. We had your fried squirrel (tastes like chicken), baked squirrel, squirrel stew, squirrel pot pie, squirrel and eggs, squirrel hash…you get the idea.

Hunting with my dad and his brothers and my grandfather was definitely a right-of-passage sort of thing for the boys in my family, but I just got to where I really didn't like killing critters. It wasn't any big anti-type-anything crusade, it's just a personal place that I came to. So long as I still buy my meat wrapped all nice and neat from the supermarket, I am not about to question what anyone else does to eat. Killing animals as trophies, that's another story … and one you are wasting your time trying to sell me on.

But, not wanting to shoot living creatures in no way meant that I hung up my guns.

Some sort of a weapon designed to propel a projectile was always a big part of my everyday life as a kid. My cousin Kenny and I would barrel through the woods behind my grandfather's place on mini-bikes or one of Pap's ponies with a BB or pellet gun tied to the seat or saddle horn. Long before Jean Shepard and 'A Christmas Story' our mothers were constantly admonishing us not to "shoot each other's eyes out'" as if it was something we may have tried had they not warned us not to.

OK, the possibility existed…

Our hunting excursions did not involve warm-blooded creatures, but rather a truly redneck activity that we called "washin' machine huntin'". This deeply intellectual pursuit involved looking for an abandoned appliance dumped back among the trees and seeing how many holes we could pump into it with the aforementioned pellet guns.

If you have never heard the sound that a metal pellet makes when it hits an old Maytag dryer…well, it's hard to describe…but it is deeply satisfying.

Our white-ware hunting days were cut short the autumn afternoon that we spotted a new slice of metal amongst the pines and opened up on it like John Wayne on Iwo Jima.

It is truly amazing how much a white, 1972 AMC Gremlin can look like an old refrigerator from a distance. I am afraid that the high school boy that had drove his girl in for a little backwoods neckin' may have been scarred for life. I don't know if he thought his date's daddy had shown up or if the county cops were cracking down on teenage sex, but he peeled outta there like his head was a-fire and his ass was a-catchin'. Flashes of bare ass were definitely glimpsed as the occupants scurried from the back to the front seats.

Once we realized that nobody was really hurt, well, I don't remember ever laughing so hard, before or since. We did give up hunting major appliances, though, and that was probably for the best.

The Louisville Slugger

Dad had been gone for about a year, and it was time to clean out the rest of his things. My sisters were going to help mom in the house getting his clothes ready for the church yard sale while their husbands and I went through the tools and assorted junk in his old shed.

I got to the home place a little before everyone else. I grabbed a cup of coffee, kissed mom, and headed out back. I wanted a moment alone among the hammers, saws, jars of nails, torn-down lawn mower engines and half-empty paint cans that still held the essence of my father. The door to the shed screeched in rusty protest as I pulled it open. It had never made so much as a squeak when dad was alive. He had kept it well oiled, and was out in his shed nearly every day. He always had about 11 projects going on that were "just about finished".

All of them were still there. In his shed. Just about finished.

I rested my coffee cup on a shelf and got on with the sad business at hand. I tossed some of dad's well-worn hand tools into an old toolbox so my brothers-in-law could sort through them. His old weed whacker was back in a corner, and I was sure one of the boys would want it, so I dug it out. There, hidden behind the oily, grassy whacker, was something that hadn't actually belonged to my dad. It was, in fact, mine. Still, it bound me to my father in a way that none of the rest of the stuff in that musty old shed ever could.

It was a Louisville Slugger, white ash. The black electrical tape dad had so carefully wrapped around the handle was unraveled, cracked and peeling. There were scuff marks on the business side from the sweet spot to the handle, but precious few on the Hillerich and Bradsby trademark side, because every boy knows that hitting on the trademark guarantees a broken bat.

The "28" stamped on the knob at the bottom was nearly scrapped away by the countless times it had been dragged across the sand of a Little League field or asphalt of a playground. I had started Little League with this bat and played with it for one, maybe two seasons until both I and the bats got bigger. In later years, I became a pretty good ball player. But when I was seven-years-old and this 28 ounce stick was my Excalibur, I suffered from the most terrible curse that can afflict a small boy.

I was afraid of the ball.

I loved baseball. I had ached for the moment when I would be old enough to play Little League ball. The day I got my first uniform, I stood in front of the mirror and admired myself for hours in my knickers, knee-socks and shirt that said 'Rebels' on the front and 'Jubb's Store' on the back.

Mom said I was going to wear my uniform out putting it on and taking it off before I ever played my first game. Dad gave me my bat the day before my first game. I could already hear the **CRACK** it would make when I launched that very first little league pitch into the stratosphere and served notice to everyone that I, a future hall-of-famer, had **ARRIVED**, baby.

I had always been a solid sandlot ballplayer, but a cruel trick of my November birthday meant that I wouldn't be playing in Little League with kids my own age. I wound up, because my birthday was late in the year, moving into the bottom of the age group above mine and playing with boys that were two and sometimes even three years older than me. They pitched hard. Really hard. Some of them could even throw the beginnings of a curveball, albeit not with much accuracy.

And that was part of the problem.

I did fine as long as the coach was lobbing fat ones at batting practice, but come game time it was a different story. I went from being a guy that was one of the best hitters on the sandlot to cowering at the plate until three strikes were called, sometimes even bailing out on a pitch that was a called strike right down the middle because I was convinced it was about to bean me.

The Slugger never left my shoulder. I began to suffer that ultimate boyhood indignity of outfielders moving in and yelling "Easy out" whenever I stepped up to the plate.

After every game, I would sit in the back of the car, fighting back tears of shame. Dad would smile into the rear-view mirror and say, "Don't worry, you'll get 'em next game."

But I knew it wasn't true.

I started to hate baseball.

I wanted to quit.
Then one evening, Dad had just come home from work and I could see he was tired, so the last thing I expected was for him to say, "Grab your bat and your glove."

We went out into the backyard and tossed the ball around a little bit. No big deal, we did that all the time. Then dad asked, "So, how's it going at the plate?"

"You know how it's going," I mumbled, "I stink."

"No, you don't stink. You're just afraid of the ball."

"I am not."

"Yes, you are, and, you know what, it's ok, even pretty smart to be a little afraid. That'll save your ass. We just gotta get you over being so afraid that you won't stay in the box. Here, throw me the ball. As hard as you can."

Dad had his glove on so I didn't think anything of it when I whipped the ball at him as hard as I could. That is, until he dropped his glove, stood up, and let the ball hit him right in the chest. He winced a bit and said, "Wow, good arm. Do it again."

"No way."

"Ray, I said throw the ball."

Boys in those days did as they were told, so I lobbed an easy one in his general direction.

He fired it back at me and said, "I said throw it. Hard."

So I let it fly. This time, instead of letting it nail him, he dropped to the ground and the ball sailed up and cracked the side of the house. Dad waved at mom when she frowned at us from the kitchen window.

"See, son. I let one hit me, and it stung a little, but it didn't kill me. I kept my eye on the other one, and it never even touched me. I've been watching. You close your eyes, just for a second, whenever the pitcher throws the ball, so you don't know where it is, and you get scared of it popping you. Now it's your turn. Just keep your eye on the ball."

I am afraid that the modern child psychologists among you will have heart failure at what happened next. All I can say is…it was one of the best lessons I ever learned.

My dad threw the ball at me.

He held my glove and bat in one hand, and whipped the Rawlings right at me with the other. Never too hard, never too fast, but hard enough and fast enough that I had to dive to get out of the way, and it stung like heck when I didn't move quite fast enough. Yeah, it stung. But it didn't kill me.

I am not about to belabor an obvious analogy here about life and stuff coming at you and learning when to duck and how to take your licks when they come. You'll have to get to that on your own.

What I learned that day was how to stay in the box and keep my eye on the ball. While some might say it was horrible to throw a baseball at a small boy, my dad knew it was much harder on me to constantly fail at something I loved so much. He had no intention of hurting me, he was teaching me, and some lessons can only come the hard way.

Maybe his methodology wouldn't pass muster in these more 'enlightened' times, but let me say this; It worked. By the time dad let me have my bat back in the fading twilight of that Baltimore evening, he was bringing the heat, and I was spraying it all over the yard. Our old house still has the broken shingles to prove it.

My first at bat at the next game, I swung on the very first pitch and launched it. No, it didn't quite make the stratosphere; in fact, it barely cleared the second baseman's head. But when the dust cleared, I was standing on first base. I looked for my dad in the wooden stands, and he smiled.

Nothing I have accomplished since that day has made me as proud as that bloop single up the middle.

Nothing.

On second thought, maybe I will make that point about hanging in the box long enough to take your licks.

When my brothers-in-law finally showed, we finished cleaning out the pieces of one very good man's life. They asked me what I wanted before they divvied up the rest. I told them they could have it all.

All except one 28 ounce piece of wood.

I Hated that Dog

And he had it in for me from day one. For 14 years, he was the canine bane of my very existence. Just hours after we first brought him home he managed to chew up my glasses. The next day, he got up onto the kitchen counter, fished the brand new replacement pair out of my briefcase and destroyed those as well. My wife said it was my fault for not locking my briefcase. She always took that stupid dog's side. He was her first baby and, brother, he knew it.

I was working nights when we first got him, and my wife convinced me she needed the company and a watch dog while I was working. The watch dog part was a bit of a stretch when you figure he was a little brown Pomeranian about the size of a coffee pot. A yapping, hairy, brownish football with legs.

My wife let her puppy sleep with her the first few nights after we brought him home, and he soon sorted out that I would put him back in his bed when I came home from work. This apparently annoyed him. He saw me as a rival for my wife's affections, and took to doing what male dogs do…marking his territory. Unfortunately, his territory happened to be my pillow. There is nothing quite like putting your head down after a long night's labor only to find it is now resting in a half-warm, half-cold puddle of puppy pee.

I hated that dog.

When the kids started coming a couple of years later, my wife was worried that he would get jealous and be mean to the children. The truth is that from the day we brought our daughter from the hospital, he sat beside her or lay under her bed, as if he knew this fragile human pup needed the protection of the big dog he always believed he was. He did exactly the same when our son was born. Ok, that's one point in his favor.

Usually, though, he was just a big pain in the ass, ears and everywhere else. He barked. Continuously. At everything. Squirrels, people, the television, random molecules…he barked at them all.

And God how he shed. Seriously, I could've supplied an order of self-flagellating monks a year's supply of hair shirts from his daily output.

He had a talent for rolling in the foulest smelling stuff he could find. He would strut proudly into the kitchen, smelling like a combination of rotten herring and whale droppings, and then look at me like I was the head warden at Angola because I had to wash him.

He also loved to eat stuff that made him sick. I think he did it on purpose, just so I had even more mess to clean up. If dogs can laugh, he was guffawing at me at every opportunity.

I hated that dog.

So, why does our house seem so empty since the Sunday a few weeks ago that we had to let him go? He had gone deaf, was moving slower and slower every day and couldn't see too well. He didn't even bark much anymore. Those last days before the end, he didn't even get out of his bed. We kept food and water next to him and prayed for a miracle, but he couldn't eat or drink. No miracles were forthcoming. Somehow, sensing his end was near I guess, he braved the steps one more time and found us all in the kitchen. He lay on my wife's lap one last time while the kids told him goodbye.

They all cried and my wife kissed her first baby farewell. I wrapped him in his tattered quilt and laid him next to me on the front seat of my old truck. As I drove to the vet, I remembered a time when he was still a puppy and my wife went home to visit her family. He was my dog for that week. We went to the drive-thru and split burgers. He sat next to me on the couch watched football and ate hot wings. I didn't even mind cleaning up the inevitable mess afterwards. When the wife got back, he tossed me over like old news, but didn't we have us a time for a while there, boy?

We buried him under a pretty tree in our backyard. I wish I could tell you he once rescued a baby from a burning building or could do Algebra while he sang and danced, but he was really nothing more or less than a damn good dog. Oh, he had it in for me from day one and caused me nothing but grief while he was here. And then, he broke my heart by leaving us.

I hated that dog.

Mothers

The plain truth is, I would not be able to wax semi-poetically about the joys of fatherhood if there wasn't a mother or two involved somewhere.

The things I have done wrong in my life are legion…epic, really. My mother would be quick to point out that these misadventures are not her fault. She just shakes her head and says, "I raised him better than that."

And she did.

Through some kind of miracle and blind pig luck I managed to make sure that my own kids have perfect moms. The mother of my oldest daughter Sandy is a wonderful woman and an exceptional mother. We are among the lucky few that have weathered divorce and remained friends. That Sandy has grown into an accomplished young woman has a whole lot more to do with her mom than with anything I have done.

I am learning to live with that.

Sometimes, one good move can make up for a whole boatload of stupid. Marrying my wife Lotte is the move that finally balanced my ledger.

She is my best friend.

Look, I know how corny that sounds…but truth is truth.

She tolerates my ageing rock star, frustrated poet nonsense and my unending, incessant "I coulda been a contender" bleating.

When I see her in the morning, I forget all about all of the things that I think I don't have and so desperately need and remember all of the ways that my life has been blessed because of her and the amazing, annoying, beautiful children we have made together.

I wish I could spin a gentle tale here about how Lotte and I rediscover each other again after a long work week by lying in bed on a Sunday morning, her head resting on my chest, drinking coffee and sharing the Sunday paper.

I could tell you all of that, but I'd be lying.

These days, we are much more likely to wake up and find ourselves separated by two kids and two dogs while Spongebob's dulcet tones assault our weary ears.

I can get a little grumpy about that.

My wife's eyes light up at the sight of her babies with a joy that I do not have the words to communicate. That light takes both my breath and my grumpiness away every time.

Anything good about anything I have ever done or ever will do is because she allows the sorry likes of me to share her life.

She is my shelter…she is my best friend...and her love is the key that unlocked my Father's Heart.

'She is my Shelter' is nothing more or less than a straight up love song to my wife. It has been recorded by other artists, but this the first time I have recorded it myself. This one's for Lotte. She truly is my shelter.

All of the songs from A Father's Heart are available at http://weaverwrites. com/songs_from_a_fathers_heart

She is My Shelter

Sleepin' late, Sunday morning,
Her head resting on my chest.
Times like this, it's easy to remember,
all of the ways that my life has been blessed.

She is right where I belong,
she keeps the secrets that I tell her.
She keeps me safe, she keeps me warm,
She is My Shelter.

Quiet words after the passion,
fingers tracing up and down her skin.
Each one of us completes the other.
No beginning and they'll be no end.

She is right where I belong,
she keeps the secrets that I tell her.
She keeps me safe, she keeps me warm,
She is My Shelter.

She is right where I belong,
she keeps the secrets that I tell her.
She keeps me safe, she keeps me warm,
She is My Shelter.

(c) 2016 Ray Weaver/Morten Wittrock

The Beautiful Game

Let's say you were working quietly at your job as, oh, I don't know, an auto mechanic and someone suddenly walked up to you and said,

"Ya know what? I think you'd make a good neurosurgeon."

I have just had a similar experience. I sent in 70 bucks (!) and signed my son up for spring soccer. Someone at the soccer office apparently took one look at Justin's application and said,

"Ya know what? I think this kid's dad is head coach material!"

OK, so what probably happened is that the league begged and pleaded with every other parent with a kid on the team and they all had to do their nails this season, so the officials took one last look at the bottom of the soccer-dad barrel - and there I was.

I know nothing about soccer. Zip. Nada. The big goose egg.

Heck, I have lived in Europe for decades and managed to remain blissfully ignorant of the beautiful game'.

I grew up in Baltimore, Maryland, where sports were defined by the Os, the Colts and the Bullets.

Period.

There was a teacher from some country where people spoke with an accent at our high school that tried to turn us on to soccer, but we red-blooded Yank kids just couldn't get behind a sport where no one ever seemed to score and games could actually end 0-0.

And there were short pants involved. What the hell kind of sport is that?

My first official move as Head Coach was to enlist my Danish wife as my assistant. The Danes have a national team, and she had actually played the game, so I figured that gave me an edge. Not to mention someone to blame when we went 0 and 10 for the season. I hit Amazon for a used copy of 'Coaching Soccer for Dumb Dads Who Should Learn When Not to Answer the Phone'.

I rented 'Bend it Like Beckham'. My wife seemed disappointed that he wasn't actually in the film.

I also called some of my English pals in a panic. Their advice was pretty much the same across the board:

"Don't call it soccer! It is football!"

Yeah, right. I'll call this game football when you lot stop putting junk in the 'boot' of your car and looking for an engine under the 'bonnet'. You wear boots on your feet and a bonnet on your head, and I already know what football is. It is a sport played by large steroidal men slamming into each other at suicidal speeds for an hour.

It involves consuming hot chicken wings and adult beverages while watching.

It is bliss.

The good news for me is finding out that most 7-year-olds know even less about soccer than I do.

They are attracted to a soccer ball the same way that electrons are pulled toward a nucleus. Where ever that ball is going, all seven of my coed warriors (including the goal keeper) are always trailing right behind.

So far, my 'coaching' has involved roaming the sidelines, drinking coffee and yelling,

"Don't bunch up" or "Find someone and cover them for Christ's…uhmm, I mean…Pete's sake".

My most important coaching duty has been arranging for after-game snacks and drinks. Did you know that every kid in America is now apparently allergic to at least one common snack food?

The one piece of consistent advice I have received from all of the books, websites - even the English has been, "Soccer is a game of passing. The team that learns how to pass will win more often than not."

I am following that excellent advice.

Oh, I don't know how well the team will do with learning to pass the actual ball, but watch me find a way to pass this snack gig off to my wife. It will indeed be a thing of beauty.

Anyway, I haven't found any junior Beckhams or Peles among my charges as of yet. Truth be told, I am not sure I'd recognize one if I had one.

But my son likes me being out there with him, and some of my best memories of my own dad involve him coaching my Little League team and believe me, the only thing he had in common with Earl Weaver was a last name.

The enthusiasm that the kids bring to the game is inspiring. At its core, soccer is pretty simple; you run, you kick the ball and you hope that it goes where you want it to go. It's fun, it is great exercise, and mostly, it gives me a few more hours with my son before he gets to that age that he'd rather be seen with last year's iPhone than his old man .

It truly is a beautiful game.

A Junkyard Christmas

My old man was not much on plumbers, electricians, garages or repair shops of any kind. As long as it was even close to possible and for as long as he could, dad fixed things himself. He was pretty good with cars, but his expertise did not extend very far into the interior of our old house. Chez Weaver was often soggy with leaky elbow joints and electrical wiring that would scare a county code inspector to death. The rig he created to get extension phones into every room of our house looked like Medusa on a bad hair day.

Like I said, dad was good with cars, but he always had his own special way of getting a repair job done; never, ever the way you or I may have done it and God forbid he actually look into the owner's manual. I am not sure the old man even knew that cars came with an owner's manual. I sure as hell never saw him look at one.

One of his greatest automotive moments came on Christmas I was 17 and we spent Christmas Eve putting a new transmission in my old car. The tranny in my '68 Chevy station wagon had finally ground itself to death and I was in complete freak-out mode that I was going to be carless at Christmas. The equation was pretty simple;

Carless = Girlfriendless = No fun under the mistletoe.

I certainly didn't have the money for a new automatic transmission, so my Christmas was looking pretty blue. Enter dad, the blue-collar Santa.

"I'll drive you to the junkyard and get you a transmission and you can help me put it in on Saturday…we'll call it your Christmas present."

"But Saturday is Christmas Eve, Dad!"

"That's the deal, take it or leave it."

A junkyard transmission for Christmas - and I get to put it in on Christmas Eve.

I don't believe Bing - or even Elvis - has a song about that one.

Saturday dawned very, very early and good, old-fashioned east coast, Chesapeake Bay, sleet-in-your-face-in December cold. We went to the junkyard and Dad haggled his best deal on my oily Christmas present and we hauled it to our backyard to put it in my Chevy.

Of course we didn't own the proper jacks or lifts. Oh, I'm sure we could have borrowed them somewhere, but dad was never one to stop in the middle of a job for a little thing like not having the right tools.

"Get me those old books from the shed, son," he said.

"What books?"

"That old set of A&P encyclopaedias we're gonna burn this winter."

Like I said, the old man never even looked at an owner's manual. What was he going to do? Look up "T" for transmission?

"What do you need encyclopaedias for, Dad?"

"Ray, just do what I say and get me the damn books."

Now, you are going to have to try and picture this -

December on the Chesapeake. Colder than your wife's feet in the middle of your back. My mission, with no choice at all as to whether I accepted it or not, was to lay upon the frozen earth, underneath my Chevy station wagon, and wedge volumes of the A&P Supermarket Illustrated Encyclopaedia, one by one, under the transmission my father was lifting by throwing all of his weight on a 6 foot long two-by-four. We had already dropped the old transmission to the ground and were using it as a fulcrum. Enough leverage (and books) would "lift that sucker up to where we can just bolt her right on. Nothin' to it, son."

It worked like a charm.

No earth science class ever gave a better demonstration of the principals of leverage, and no set of crummy supermarket encyclopaedias were ever put to better use. They also got pretty soaked with transmission fluid, so they "burned real good" too. We used them as kindling all winter.

I do not, in these more enlightened times, recommend automatic transmission fluid as a fire starter. But it was a different world then, and my old man didn't waste anything.

I think the song 'Half the Man' is the oldest one included here. My dad was still alive when I wrote it, and I'm glad he had the chance to hear it. I have tried over the years to rewrite it so it would be shorter and perhaps more commercial and maybe find a nice lucrative home with a Nashville artist. In the end, it always wanted to be just what it is; a somewhat corny but honest and heartfelt declaration of love from a son to his father.

All of the songs from A Father's Heart are available at http://weaverwrites. com/songs_from_a_fathers_heart

Half the Man

My daddy made it out of high school, he was workin' by
the time he turned 14,
Used to hear him leavin' out every morning, 40 years he
ran that damn machine.
He never found his fortune, he was just a workin' man,
If I was half the man my daddy was, I'd be twice the man I
am.

He taught me all a poor man's lessons, about lovin' Jesus
and your family.
How to keep this old truck runnin', nothin' worth havin'
comes for free.
He taught me how to love a woman, by the way he held
my momma's hand,
If I was half the man my daddy was, I'd be twice the man I
am.

The lines around his eyes had gotten deeper, I think he'd
lost a step or two.
He said the hardest thing about gettin' old is when you
can't do the things you used to do.
In my eyes he was a hero, a strong but gentle man.
If I was half the man my daddy was, I'd be twice the man I
am.

Watched his babies all from up and leave him, and bring
him home some babies of their own.
He took a flower every Sunday, to where his angel slept
beside her stone.
He knew that one day he would join her, and they'd turn
for home again.

If I was half the man my daddy was, I'd be twice the man I am.
I'd be twice the man I am.

All of the songs from A Father's Heart are available at http://weaverwrites. com/songs_from_a_fathers_heart

The Letter Birds

I have been sitting on your bed for a while since you headed off to schoolI hope you don't mind.

I am holding your pillow close to my face as I look around your room, safe and warm in the scent of your little girl dreams. Like the girl who lives here, this room is a work in progress. The Lion King, Aladdin and Nemo still occupy most of the real estate on the walls. Lately, though, some of that valuable space has been taken up by the Backstreet Boys, 'NSYNC, Justin Timberlake and some handsome young men that call themselves "Blue". Now, Disney's finest are not giving up without a fight. They still maintain control over the DVD machine, but the boy bands are definitely staking their claim to the CD player.

Alas, there is no sign of Barney these days, and I fear he has suffered the same fate as the colorful clowns I hung up before you were born. Taken down, boxed-up and flea-marketed. Who could have known you would be born petrified of clowns? Then again, who would have believed you would ever say goodbye to Barney?

How we sang those safe, silly songs while the big purple dude was still the king of your world. In the house, in the car, at the beach, on airplanes - much to the delight of the other passengers, I'm sure - you would punch the big red button on your first cassette player and sing them and sing them and sing them until I would roll my eyes and plead, "Not again, Sandy. PLEASE. Not again." And then of course, we sang them again.

I think it was tough for you to let the old boy go.

Was it really just last winter that we were snowed in, and all of the old Barney videos suddenly reappeared? "The Ants go Marching One-by-One" enjoyed one big last hurrah in our house. That sweet, snowy day, along with these crazy mixed-up walls of pop stars and cartoon lions, make me think that you have inherited your dad's sentimental heart. You feel life's natural tug to grow and move on, but you are afraid to leave anyone or anything behind. Even big purple dinosaurs.

Fear not, sweet girl, for in your short years with us you have already outgrown many things, things you may even have forgotten, but your sentimental old dad has a box in his heart for each and every one of them.

You may never sit and talk again for hours about the "bod-a-wees" and "dader-daders", but I remember those folks well. They moved in with us sometime during your second year, and moved on again about the time you started kindergarten. I have no idea from what childhood well these mythical characters sprang, but while they lived with us you gave them a deep, rich history. There were entire lands filled with kings and queens and damsels in distress.

What adventures they had! It's been a while since I have heard from them. I hope they are well.

We rarely used baby talk in our house, but your ears-in-training heard oatmeal as "opeo" and pancakes as "pamcakes". Even long after you had learned the correct pronunciations, I would ask, almost every morning, "So what's for breakfast, kiddo, opeo or pamcakes?" You would always giggle and reply with one of your little girl versions. This morning, though, when I once again posed our silly morning question you replied, "Puhlease, Dad, it is *oatmeal* or *pancakes*, and anyway, I want a soft-boiled egg."

So, I guess even the letter birds will be leaving us soon. I remember the first time you noticed that the geese winging their way south below the gray autumn clouds etched ragged 'V's' and 'W's' across the sky. You pointed up and said, "See daddy, letter birds, letter birds, the birds can make letters!"

And we have called them letter birds ever since.

Soon, far too soon for me anyway, they will become simply geese again. I'll lock away the letter birds in that same wistful place I keep the bod-a-wee's and opeo and pamcakes, the Lion King and his pals…and good ol', dopey Barney.

I know it is the way things must be, just as I know that there are new and even better days and memories yet to come.

So, give me a break for sounding like an old waterhead. It's just that for each and every box I tape up and put away in my heart, I can feel you letting go of just a little more of my hand.

Godspeed, Sandy

My oldest daughter turns 21 next month. I do not know when that happened. I just looked up one day and there was a woman standing where my little girl had been.

If I didn't think she would laugh out loud at her mushy, sentimental dad, this is what I would tell her…

"Why, just a moment ago, you were strolling through the living room wearing your tattered nighty-night blanket as a cape and Winnie the Pooh footy pajamas. You were pushing a toy plastic shopping cart crammed with stuffed animals in front of the TV so we could all enjoy watching the Never Ending Story together for the 2,000,007th time."

I swear it was just yesterday that I was teaching you how to write your name, and now, all of a sudden, you're a marketing major in college and, truth be told, you write better than your old man.

You used to lay out a gourmet tea party spread of Oreo Cookies and Kool-Aid tea that you made "all by myself ".

When you visited last weekend you lectured me on the importance of organic food and hassled me about cutting back on my burger runs.

In my mind, I still see a little red-haired girl with chubby cheeks and legs and a smile that takes my breath away.

The smile remains, but the chubby little girl has grown into a statuesque woman with looks that literally stop people in their tracks. It makes me proud and scares the hell out of me at the same time.

Your mom and I divorced when you were little, so your eyes always hold just a trace of wistfulness for the moments that we lost, but you have the self-assurance of someone who learned early that sometimes the breaks go the wrong way and you have to learn to roll with the punches.

The fact that I have something to do with both your sadness and your strength is the source of my greatest sadness and my greatest joy.

You were my first baby and now you are an adult and, no, I am not ready.

I want more long summer days, making sand castles on a windswept beach, jumping waves, eating French fries and pizza and molasses paddles.

I want to swim off the rocks one more time at our secret spot along the Danish coastline and stop along the side of the road for fresh black cherries and spit the pits out of the car window.

I want a few more rides on the roller coaster when the fear in your eyes is kept at bay by the knowledge that your dad would never, ever let anything hurt you.

I want another evening of talent shows featuring 'Hot Crossed Buns' and 'Three Blind Mice' on the recorder. I promise not to mention, the way I didn't mention the first time around, that the two songs are pretty much the same, and I promise to clap like it is opening night at Carnegie Hall.

I want to feel that wonderful shock of recognition I had as I watched you dance onstage for the first time. The lithe, beautiful woman I saw that night bore little resemblance to the tumble-down princess that single-handedly kept Neosporin in business for a decade or so, but they are both my beautiful daughter.

I want to run down the road behind you just one more time, breathlessly holding onto your bicycle seat until you find your balance and take off on your own.

You have found your own balance, Sandy.

Godspeed.

'Princess Years' is probably the song of mine that gets the most visceral reaction when I play it live. Large, scary looking men with shaved heads and tattoos on their faces come up with tears in their eyes to tell me that they have daughters and that listening to the song "really f*cked them up". I guess sometimes the most personal story can be the most universal.

All of the songs from A Father's Heart are available at http://weaverwrites.
com/songs_from_a_fathers_heart

Princess Years

She held back her tears, but I felt her heart break,
when I told her I was going away.
I said, "Nothing will change." We both knew better,
when I turned around, I heard her say.

"Daddy, who'll chase the monsters from under my bed?
Who will play baseball with me?
How will I know where to send the invitation,
to invite the prince to tea?"

White lace dresses, for mademoiselle,
Daddy look what I made, all by myself.
Oreo cookies, Kool-aid tea.
For only two guests, the princess and me.
I'd give up my life to dry just one of her tears,
and have back her Princess Years.

We'd sit with our cups on her bedroom floor,
she stand on my feet, and we'd dance.
A little girl's dreams turned her dad into a prince,
and her room into a castle in France.

White lace dresses, for mademoiselle,
Daddy look what I made, all by myself.
Oreo cookies, Kool-aid tea.
For only two guests, the princess and me.
I'd give up my life to dry just one of her tears,

and have back her Princess Years.

'cross the years and the miles, came an invitation,
from the princess to her wedding day.
The end of a childhood I let slip through my fingers,
"Daddy will you come to give me away?"

No fairy tale wedding ever imagined,
ever saw a more beautiful bride.
Trembled as I gave my little girl's hand,
to the handsome prince now by her side.

White lace dresses, for mademoiselle.
"Daddy look what I made … a life for myself."
A room full of guests stand up to see,
one more minuet for the princess and me.
She stepped up on my feet and smiled through her tears,
and forgave me her Princess Years.

(c) 2016 Ray Weaver/Morten Wittrock

All of the songs from A Father's Heart are available at
http://weaverwrites.
com/songs_from_a_fathers_heart

C'mon and Safari with Me

A wise man once said, "A woman has the last word in any argument. Anything a man says after that word is simply the beginning of the next argument".

My wife and I have the usual amount of marital disagreements when it comes to raising the kids. I have learned, finally, that the best way to settle those discussions quickly is to accept that I am never, ever going to have the last word.

The kids realized this early on. If there is a dispute to be settled or a question to be answered they bypass me completely and ask mom.

Mom is omnipotent.

Me, I am kind of like an old Commodore 64 computer; there may be information in here, but it's probably corrupted and nobody has a clue how to get to it.

One thing my wife and I do agree on is that kids these days have too much stuff. Play Stations, Xboxes, DVD players, iPads, iPhones iCan'tkeeptrackofitall…the list is endless, and every time they change the color or add a new widget to one of these things, why the poor child simply MUST have the latest version or they will seem as hopelessly dinosaur-like as the aforementioned Commodore 64 and will suffer intense peer group ridicule and public humiliation.

We decided - ok, she decided and I agreed - to get off the electronics merry-go-round and start giving the kids "adventures and experiences" rather than things for birthdays.

This seemed like an excellent idea until I realized that I was actually expected to take part in these adventures. Suddenly an Xbox seems like the perfect birthday gift!

A recent Weaver family birthday excursion involved the entire brood taking surfing lessons on my son Justin's birthday.

We all love the ocean, and, over the years, I have often thought of taking surfing lessons myself. I handled it the way I always deal with such urges; I took a nice nap on the beach until it passed.

This time, though, there I was in all my 50ish glory, on the beach at Ocean City, Maryland at some ridiculous hour of the morning - the Thraser's French Fry stand wasn't even open - with my yoga-fit wife, my athletic son and my graceful 12 year-old daughter.

My oldest daughter wisely decided to watch this latest excursion from the safe distance of Nashville, Tennessee away.

The annoyingly handsome and ridiculously young surfing instructors could not have been nicer. They coached my family through the basics of standing up on a surf board and pushed us into the waves so each of us had a shot at getting at least one good ride during the one hour lesson. My son caught on quickly and actually stood up on his second or third try. My wife rode a wave all the way into the beach and the 12-year-old was skittering on top of the waves like a dragonfly in no time.

To say that surfing didn't go well for me brings a whole new meaning to the concept of 'understatement'.

No Flinstone's episode of Fred attempting to surf was ever as funny, and never have one man's family and two surfing instructors labored so hard not to laugh.

Every time I finished a 'ride', I noticed that the instructors all of a sudden needed to dive under water to, Oh, I don't know, fix their bleached-blonde perfect hair or search for hermit crabs.

Did you know that the sound of howling laughter actually carries under water?

My wife did her best to salvage my dwindling dignity, but every, "Nice try, honey" or "Almost" was accompanied by a face that we all recognize.

Remember the classic Mary Tyler Moore Show episode when Chuckles the Clown dies and every one at the funeral is trying not to laugh?

That face.

A little song, a little dance, a ton of beach sand down my pants.

I did stand up once for the briefest of nano-seconds. OK, truth being told, I was falling forward and the momentum carried my body into an semi-upright position.

I did learn an important lesson, though. The higher your head goes above the surfboard, the greater the distance it will have to go to make contact with the sand when you fall. You also get a lot of water up your nose. My nasal cavities were still dripping salt water the next day.

I think my son will remember it as one of the best birthday's ever, and he fell in love with the sport. This of course means that he wants me to buy him a surfboard.

Oh well, at least it won't have to be plugged in, recharged or rebooted

The Beat Goes On

My daughter Savannah is a musician. God help her. The poor kid never had a chance.

I have been beating my heart up against the music business for the better part of my life, and her mom is the best non-performing musician I know. In fact, I fell in love with the sound of my wife before anything else. In a scene that seems hopelessly romantic, highly improbable and yet is absolutely true, I used to hear my wife playing a wooden flute through the window of my small Danish hotel room before we really knew each other. She would sit out on her balcony and play every morning. The sound of her music blending with the waves crashing against the rocks below my window, and yeah, the blonde hair, blue eyes and perfect smile…

Anyway, back to Savannah. She has always loved music. When she was an infant, we battled her colic to the sounds of Martina McBride's "Wild Angels" CD. It was the only one that worked.

When she got a little older, she went nowhere without her Fisher Price tape player and a tape her grandfather had made her called "Granddad's Music." It was a collection of old rock and roll hits by the original artists, but in Savannah's mind, since it was called "Granddad's Music", it, quite logically, must have been her grandfather performing all of the songs by Chuck Berry, the Platters, the Drifters and Herman's Hermits. Talented guy, my father-in-law.

I guess the first inkling that something special was going on with Savannah and music was when some musicians we were sharing a house with one summer asked me when I was going to do something about "that kid's singing". Apparently she was standing in a small yard behind the house every morning and giving, a cappella, a one or two hour concert of Dolly Parton's Greatest Hits every day.

She was four-years-old.

These world-weary, grizzled music vets weren't complaining about the noise. They were totally charmed by her pitch perfect performance. They would open the windows to listen and they told me, "This is something special."

She has the gift…and she has the fever. I listen with a mixture of envy and fear as the music flows through her and I watch the awareness dawn in her eyes as she works it all out. She knows how the chords go together and the melody rests inside. She hears the beat and the syncopation and intuits how the words weave in between. It is an awareness like no other to a musician, it touches all of the senses. She can literally hear, taste, feel and smell the music.

I envy her because I know I will never experience that rush again in exactly the same way, and I am afraid for her because I know how hard the music business is. Music will be her greatest joy and her deepest heartbreak.

She has been writing her own songs for as long as I can remember and has gone well past the "That's a cute little girl song" stage and into the intangible. The songs are good. The lyrics come from a well I certainly didn't have as a teenager and the melodies are professional, tight and complex. Soon she is going to play a song, baring her heart and her soul, to some fat jerk behind a desk that wouldn't know a good song if it bit him on his ass and he'll turn it off after 15 seconds and say, "Got anything else, kid?"

Or she'll be singing her truth in a club somewhere and have some inebriated slug ask, in the middle of her song, of course, "Don't you know any Buffett, girly?"

It comes with the territory.

Because she is a woman, she is going to have an extra layer of nonsense to wade through. But she will also have those precious, magical moments when everything is in tune, the universe aligned and she'll look out and see someone she has never met singing along with a song she has written. That's as close to perfect as it gets.

I get scared for her, but I am also recapturing a bit of my own youth watching her sense of wonder and excitement. For many years, the music biz made me angry. Lost deals, missed chances and "I coulda been a contenders" clouded my vision.

Not too long ago, I had all of my kids gathered together in one spot, and my wife was sitting next to me, and I realized that all of the good things in my life had come my way because I learned four chords and a few variations and slapped a few clever couplets on top of them.
Music has given me my life. It has been a hard life, sure, but it has been a fine and rich life. Minus some of the hard stuff, I wish my Savannah the same.

Rock on, baby, rock on.

Universal Languages

Through the sort of modern miracles that exist somewhere just beyond my comprehension, I am writing this story on a laptop while sitting in a tent on a small Danish island.

Through the tent window, a quiet Baltic breeze carries the laughter of children on the beach. Somewhere in the mix, I can hear my own two kids joining in. There are children from several countries playing and swimming on this summer beach, and do you know what the difference in the sound of their laughter is?

Nothing.

Nada.

Nothing at all.

Although I am sure, like any parent is sure, that I can immediately distinguish the sound of my own children's laughter, the truth is that be they Danish, German, Swedish, Polish, American…whatever…the high-pitched squeals of little girls and joyful noises of little boys are the same in any language. Regardless of nationality, kids are kids.

Many of the children within my earshot do not even speak the same language, but they manage to rip, race, organize

games, play soccer and hide-and-go-seek or tag together...
no translation required.

It is only when we become adults that we cover ourselves
with the prejudices and politics that cause us to carry
placards covered in hateful messages and rail at each other
on talk radio and out in the streets.

Think about it. Have you ever heard a kid use a racial slur
or make a prejudiced remark that he hadn't picked up from
an adult? Be careful what you say up there in the front
seat, Daddy, because kid's car seats are apparently
equipped with radar gear that would give the NSA a run
for their money.

If all of my traveling has taught me nothing else, it has
shown me that we are all pretty much the same in our
hearts and under our skin. We have the same dreams and
desires, especially for the generation we are leaving
behind. We want our children to be as comfortable as
possible, live in a decent home in a good town and we
want them to have a future. Mostly, we want them to be
better off than we were when we started out.

We share the same joys and bear the same sorrows. When
a mine collapses and men are trapped, whether that mine is
in China or West Virginia, mothers pray and children cry.

The sound of hearts breaking is the same the world over.

I hope my kids are making friends out there on that summer beach; the kind that you promise to stay in touch with over the winter but almost never do. As they get older, those friendships might even turn into sweet, hand-holding, first-kiss summertime romances. The kind that, like the sun, seem to come in June and wane as August fades into September. Maybe a handsome German boy will have a wistful memory of my half-Danish, half-American daughter at the same time she thinks of him and smiles.

That's another emotion that feels the same, everywhere, every time.

'Jeg Elsker Dig' is another song I wrote about my wife Lotte. She is Danish, and the song is a musical version of how we met on a tiny Danish island. 'Jeg elsker dig' means 'I love you' in Danish. My own Danish was pretty bad when I recorded it, so I often cringe when I hear the song now, but there is a certain honesty to my bad pronunciation. It really is how it sounded the first time I said those words in Danish, I guess. Hell, truth be told, I've stumbled over that phrase in English a time or two as well...

All of the songs from A Father's Heart are available at http://weaverwrites. com/songs_from_a_fathers_heart

Jeg Elsker Dig

I don't speak your language, I can only use the language of the heart.
I hope I can manage, to say the simple phrases I've been taught.
I ask your friend to tell me, the way to tell what's been on my mind.
She smiled and told me these words, I'm not sure I can say it, but I'll try.

Jeg Elsker Dig, I love you so
Jeg vil sauvner dig, I'll miss you when I go.
Farvel. Vi ses igen,
I hope I never learn to say goodbye,
Jeg Elsker Dig.

The moment that I saw you, your hair spun with gold from a midnight sun.
I'm not sure how, but you knew, I was lost and a long, long way from home.
High above a rocky coastline, reflected in the light from Christiansø,
we made love as the sun came up, it was in that moment that I knew.

Jeg Elsker Dig. I love you so
Jeg vil sauvner dig, I'll miss you when I go.
Farvel. Vi ses igen,

I hope I never learn to say goodbye,
Jeg Elsker Dig.

I know I'll find the way to make you understand,
the words I'm trying to say if you'll just take my hand.

Jeg Elsker Dig, I love you so
Jeg vil sauvner dig, I'll miss you when I go.
Farvel. Vi ses igen,
I hope I never learn to say goodbye,
Jeg Elsker Dig.

*All of the songs from A Father's Heart are available at http://weaverwrites.
com/songs_from_a_fathers_heart*

Sandy's Wedding

Sandy and Lyle were getting married. Well, they hadn't officially set a date, but we all knew it was bound to happen. Even my folks seemed resigned to it. Sandy was almost 18, so if they tried to stop her, she'd more than likely just wait a few months and get hitched anyway.

My sister had a mind of her own. Besides, Sandy had wrapped my dad around her little finger on the day she was born. He took one look at her raven hair and ocean blue eyes and was her's forever. As the years went on, she would have pretty much the same effect on just about every boy she knew, including, to my eternal annoyance, most of my friends. Deep down, I knew she was beautiful. Well, as beautiful as an annoying kid sister could be, anyway.

Actually, as far as my sister's boyfriends went, I thought Lyle was OK. Now, to be charitable, Lyle was not exactly what you would call a heartbreaker. He was a little older than Sandy (my dad said too old), skinny, with big, black horn-rimmed glasses. He was completely different and yet, in an odd way, exactly the same as all of Sandy's boyfriends. My dad took one look at him, shook his head and said, "She's brought home another stray."

He was constantly amazed that his beautiful daughter had such a knack for collecting such driftwood when it came to men. Sandy seemed oblivious to the football stars and pretty boys that would have given their eye teeth for just one date and took up with the guys that most of her friends would not have touched with a clothes pole. To me, Lyle was a step up from the guys that Sandy usually brought home. At the very least, he seemed capable of more than a two-word conversation, which is more than I could say for most of them…especially her ex-boyfriend, Jimmy.

Jimmy couldn't manage much more than a mumbled, "Sandy there?" when he called on the phone. Whenever he visited he reeked of oil, gasoline and cigarette smoke from the garage where he worked. That is, if he even bothered to come in the house at all. Mostly, he just blew his horn, and waited for Sandy in the driveway.

Dad would grunt, "Lover boy's here."

"He's just shy, Daddy," Sandy would say, kiss him on the cheek and run out the door.

That girl owned my dad.

Sandy and Jimmy had been sweethearts all through high school, and our family had endured God-only-knew how many tearful break-ups and joyful reconciliations. We'd hear raised voices, Jimmy's Ford tearing off into the night and then wait for the inevitable phone calls to start. Ten calls. Twenty. Thirty seven. Finally, dad would make her take the phone, Jimmy'd apologise and she'd take him back. It was all pretty nauseating. I couldn't figure out what she saw in the guy, and I let her know it.

So, how did we get from Jimmy and Sandy to Sandy and Lyle and impending wedding bells?

The way I heard it was that Lyle started stopping in every morning at the little bakery where Sandy worked, and after a few dozen donuts (and a few dozen rejections), he finally caught her in the middle of a breakup with Jimmy. So, Sandy went out with Lyle, and, wonder of wonders, she kept on going out with Lyle. She and Jimmy seemed finished for good this time.

Sandy started putting things into a wooden box she called her hope chest. Flatware, dishtowels, blankets…

"You're gonna need a much bigger hope chest than the one you have, as long as you'll be hoping for someone to marry you," I teased.

"Ah, come on, big brother, maybe you can dance at my wedding," she teased back.

I was still smarting from missing my senior prom because I was fundamentally and totally petrified of dancing, and she knew it.

"Hah, I'll be in a wheelchair by then," I replied weakly.

Maybe she figured she owed Jimmy a decent goodbye. Or maybe he just wore her down by constantly calling her at work and the house. Either way, Sandy agreed to meet with him "one more time".
"If Lyle calls, please DON'T tell him where I am, ok?"

"Look, don't drag me into this, Sandy. Why are you messing around with Jimmy again, anyway? Lyle's a good guy," I said.

"I am not 'messing around' with anybody. We're just going for a ride. I know you don't like him, but he's got a good heart and we were together a long time. I think I owe him that much."

That was my sister. All heart. Sandy and her strays...

The cop told my dad that Jimmy's car hit the overpass doing at least 90. The typical small town rumors flew. Alcohol. Anger. Drugs. None of it mattered. My sister and Jimmy were gone. There wasn't going to be a wedding to Lyle.

Or Jimmy.

Or anyone.

Ever.

In Sandy's hope chest I found a Kodak envelope filled with pictures of she and Lyle in Florida. Apparently, after Dad had refused to give her permission to go, she had used the story of spending the weekend with a girlfriend to sneak away. My mom knew. Moms always know, I think. She smiled sadly at the images of her lost little girl wearing Mickey Mouse ears and giant plastic sunglasses and said, "She told us she was at Dianne's that weekend, but she came home crying and said she was breaking up with Lyle. When I asked her why, she just said 'Mom, he's not as nice as he looks. Sometimes…I just miss my Jimmy."

I never saw Lyle again after my sister's funeral, so I never had a chance to ask him what Sandy meant by that.

So, I don't know…maybe all of the stuff in Sandy's hope chest was for her life with Jimmy after all. Maybe, in her heart of hearts, he was always the one she was hoping for. I remembered that she once told me, "Jimmy'd be great if he would just grow up a little."

Jimmy never had to grow up.

Neither did Sandy.

Forever seventeen.

It was a long time ago, and most days, I have forgiven Jimmy for taking my sister. His grave is just a few feet away from Sandy's, and when I visit her, I give him a nod now and then.

A nod.

Not a prayer…not just yet, Jimmy, not just yet.

On most days, I have forgiven my sister for choosing such lousy boyfriends, and robbing herself, and all of us, of the rest of her life. She was a good kid. She deserved better. She deserved a good man and a house full of kids of her own. My faith helps me believe that she will have all of that somewhere, and I'll see them when Sandy and I meet again.

And I hope that someday, somewhere, in that place where all things are possible, I finally get to dance at Sandy's wedding.

The Crab Feast

"Do they bite, Pap?"

My grandfather smiled brightly at my six-year-old cousin
Ricky and said,

"Stick your finger there in the basket and see for y'self,
boy."

It was the same answer he had given me a few years
before. Pap was a big believer in "learning by doing".

Well, it was a dumb question.

Of course they bit.

Hard.

Why else would Pap be wearing heavy black rubber gloves
in the soggy heat of a way-down-in-August Maryland
Saturday afternoon?

Even the ever-present Camel stuck to his lower lip looked
sweaty as he pulled the Chesapeake Bay blue crabs from a
wooden bushel basket and threw them into our stained old
steaming pot. Every once in a while, a sharp claw would
work its way through Pap's glove, and he would address
the crab in question in language little boys probably

shouldn't hear. Some would have doused the crabs in cold water or stabbed them through the shell with an ice pick to slow them down. Not Pap. Pap was particular about crabs, and saw to them his way. Cussin' and all.

Before tossing in the crabs, Pap had placed a wire rack in the bottom of the pot and poured in just enough water and apple-cider vinegar to reach the bottom of the rack.

"We don't boil crabs in Merlin', Raymie…we steam'em," Pap said. "Boil 'em down in Virginny…ain't worth eatin'…goddamn waste of a good crab."

Each time he got a layer of crabs in the pot, he would sprinkle in about half-a-coffecupful of Old Bay Seafood Seasoning mixed with rock salt, then another layer of crabs, more Old Bay, on up to the top. Pap liked his crabs spicy. Your lips should burn while you were eating them. Before putting on the lid, he looked around slyly and said,

"Now, don't tell your Grandma." Then he dumped in half-a-bottle of National Beer.

"Secret ingredient," he winked.

"Now, get that on in the kitchen. We got two more pots left t' do."

A pot filled with big hard crabs is a heavy load for a twelve-year-old boy, but I wasn't about to let Pap know, so I wrestled it as best I could up the back steps. When my grandmother saw me coming, she yelled through the screen,

"Herb, are you tryin' to give the boy a hernia? Here, Raymie, just set it up on the stove. Did Pappy remember the beer? Makes 'em taste better, so they say."

Pap, my dad, his brothers and I had crossed the Chesapeake Bay Bridge before dawn to 'go crabbin'' on Maryland's Eastern Shore. At daybreak, we found we had hit the weather and tides just right and we caught over two and a half bushels of keepers in a few hours.

Some people did their crabbing from piers, with traps or hand lines using old chicken necks and chopped up eels as bait. To us, river-born, that was crabbing for sissified city folk. We rowed our old wooden boat out to where the crabs lived, and then walked knee-deep in the briny bay water with bushel baskets floating in inner tubes tied to our belts. We flushed the crabs out of the seaweed with long-handled nets and dipped them up into the baskets behind us.

While the men were on their safari through Chesapeake sea weed, the women were busy at home covering the two long wooden picnic tables under the oak tree in the backyard with last week's editions of the Baltimore News

American. They had also carried the small breakfast table out of the kitchen and covered it up. That was the kid's table. A pile of mismatched butter knives lay on each table. They were for cracking and picking the crabs. Some folks had actual crab mallets with little knives built into the handle, but we weren't quite that uptown.

When the blue crabs were steamed to a bright red, Pap put the kitchen radio up in the window and tuned to WBAL and the Orioles. They were always just a game or two behind the Yankees. I hated the Yankees when I was a kid.

Still do.

The steaming pots of crabs were dumped straight onto the newspaper, and I took my place alongside my sisters and cousins at the kid's table.

Along with the crabs, there were oleo-drenched platters of late sweet corn pulled fresh that morning from the rows behind the house. Some of the ears had gashes where corn worms had been cut out.

There were Tupperware pitchers filled with sweet tea, and steel coolers packed with ice and Coca-Cola in little green glass bottles, the way God intended Coke to be.

My family was old-fashioned.

All of the men were beer drinkers, but there was never beer at family gatherings when the kids were around. That was for later, in the garage, when the kids were in bed and the men played penny poker and drank PBR and Natty Boh.

Crabs are messy, so the women and girls wore sleeveless shirts and old shorts, and the men and boys got down to their cut-offs and t-shirts or no shirts at all.

Everybody had their own way of picking and eating. Pap picked two or three crabs clean until he had a good pile of meat built up. Then he would butter a piece of Blue Ribbon bread and make a kind of crab sandwich.

My mom liked hers with saltine crackers.

I wasn't that patient. I yanked off the shell, carefully scraped out the 'Devil', which is what we called the gills (and, as every Maryland kid knew, was certain death if eaten), cleaned out the innards, broke the crab in half, snapped off a back fin and stuck the clump of meat straight into my mouth.

It takes awhile to enjoy steamed crabs. We took all afternoon. Neighbors would slow down, honk and wave as they drove by. We all waved back, even if we couldn't tell right off who was doing the honking. It was sure to be someone we knew.

Around the kid's table, the talk lately seemed to be less about baby dolls and BB guns, and more about make-up and cars, cute boys and pretty girls, and the Beatles.

Rumor had it that my sister Sandy had been seen holding hands with a football player after Friday night's game.

I myself had been writing smoldering love notes to Kathy Williams. I tore them up as soon as they were finished, but I was writing them.

Soon, nervous, silent boys would appear next to my sisters and girl cousins, and nervous, chatty girls would be perched next to me and the other boys at the table, and our family gatherings would start to feel different somehow.

On this late summer's day, though, it was still just 'us kids', together for a little while longer at the kid's table, right next to and worlds away from our parents.

The hot, lazy sun drifted west, the Orioles discovered yet another way to lose to the Yankees, and everyone ate their fill. If they didn't, it was their own darn fault, as my grandma would say.

We cleaned off the tables, took the garbage down to the pigpen, and collected the leftover crabs for soup the next day. We washed our hands in the freezing water from the hand pump at the well, and washed the day's feast down with a Popsicle.

Soon, lightning bugs would appear, and we kids would run through the cornfields and catch them in Mason jars. The old house had no air-conditioning, so it was cooler outside, and even the grown-ups would stay out for a while on this night, sitting and smoking and talking grownup talk, until the mosquitoes finally drove everyone inside.

'Grandma's Place' is another early song that I tried to rewrite a million times to get it into a more 'standard' format. It just wouldn't cooperate. It wanted to tell this story in this way.

All of the songs from A Father's Heart are available at http://weaverwrites. com/songs_from_a_fathers_heart

Grandma's Place

Last time I went home to be with my grandma, the home place was all but gone,
Shopping centres standing where we used to pick berries and new houses where our horses would run.
I guess in a while, it'll fade to a memory, then be forgotten before too long.
So before she's called home to be with my grandpa, I want to finish my grandma's song.

My grandma's house was the first one they built here, grandpa built it with his own two hands.
He loved my grandma, he loved his children, and God knows how he loved this land.
He left this world from this house that he'd lived in with my grandma right by his side.
And they tell me that Jesus came down to this house to be with grandpa on the night that he died.

So Lord, when I die, don't take me to heaven, let somebody else fill that space.
Just set my feet down on a road I remember, and I'll walk up to my
Grandma's Place.

Every winter the snow would fill up these fields, and we'd run 'til we couldn't run no more.

And dry our wet clothes on a grate above the fire and talk
with grandma while we'd played on the floor.
Grandpa'd come in with his pipe and his paper, you could
smell cherry smoke fill the air.
I could not understand when it was time to go home,
'cause I knew I was already there.

Come the summer I'd stay over and sleep in the same bed
that was my daddy's when he was a boy, and spend hours
just looking at his childhood treasures and laughin' at all
his old toys.
My sisters would pick violets to give to my grandma that
she'd sit in an old Mason jar.
We'd run chasin' fireflies through these cornfields at night,
'til one night I ran off too far.

So Lord, when I die, don't take me to heaven, let
somebody else fill that space.
Just set my feet down on a road I remember, and I'll walk
up to my
Grandma's Place.

Someday soon, I'll head back for Sunday dinner, and
grandma will ask me to give grace.
Or we'll get together on a hot summer morning, to put a
coat of paint on the old home place.
Then we'll sit in the shade of that big tree out back, and
listen while the evenin' settles in.

I'm lookin' forward to that warm summer morning when I can talk to grandma again.

So Lord, when I die, don't take me to heaven, let somebody else fill that space.
Just set my feet down on a road I remember, and I'll walk up to my
Grandma's Place.

So Lord, when I die, don't take me to heaven, let somebody else fill that space.
Just set my feet down on a road I remember, and I'll walk up to my
Grandma's Place.

So Lord, when I die, don't take me to heaven, let somebody else fill that space.Just set my feet down on a road I remember, and I'll walk up to my Grandma's Place.

(c) 2016 Ray Weaver

All of the songs from A Father's Heart are available at http://weaverwrites. com/songs_from_a_fathers_heart

Of Fathers and Sons

I like to take naps with my son. I was never much of a napper before Justin came along. Not because I don't like to sleep. Me, I love to sleep. There just never seemed to be enough time for weekday naps before. These days, when I can, I make the time.

Honestly, the things we endure for our kids.

My two girls went down for their afternoon naps without too much of a fuss. Oh, Sandy and Savannah have both had their share of night frights, but midday naps came pretty easily. Justin has always needed someone to lay down with him. I work nights and am at home during the day, so I got into the habit of doing it. (Note to the child psychologists currently reading this and shaking their heads; Yes, I know all of the reasons why the aforementioned napping with my son is supposedly 'wrong', and, no, I don't give a rat's ass what you think.)

We lie together on his bed, and he tells me what he did in kindergarten, what he had for lunch, what kids he played with, what kids pulled his hair, whose hair he pulled, and before too long, he drifts off. Unless, as sometimes happens…OK, as often happens, I zone out first. Then he whacks me and tells me I am making that "tractor noise."

I think it is the scent that gets to me. Resting there, next to my little boy, who smells exactly the way a little boy should smell; a little grass here, a little sand there, a little Nugga (the dog), and something underneath it all that is just…Justin. Hell, if the sleeping tablet folks could bottle that up, I can promise you there'd be no such affliction as insomnia.

He is, by the way, defiantly 'Justin' right now. If I say, "Come on, Spiderman (or Batman or Simba or Buzz Lightyear…based on whatever DVD is currently on constant repeat in the living room), let's go take a nap." He will dig in his heels and say, "Jeg hedder ikke Spiderman, jeg hedder Justin." ("My name is not Spiderman, my name is Justin.")

See, he is currently only speaking Danish. Oh, he can speak English, and he understands everything I say to him, and he ignores me as completely as any three-year old can ignore his father in any language. His chosen tongue of the moment, however, is Danish. He talks like mommy.

I could make a bad joke here about the "Mother Tongue"…but I won't….

Usually lying with Justin conjures up only the best kinds of images. Days we have spent together, playing ball, digging in the sand at the beach, sneaking off for hotdogs at lunch so that his sorta-vegetarian-low-fat-mom won't find out and make us, "Have some vegetables with that!" You know, Dad-and-Son stuff.

Sorry, no girls allowed.

I look at him sleeping and think, as dads do, about his future. Will he play soccer or baseball? Will he be good at math like his mom, or barely be able to make change like me? Will he learn to love music the way Savannah does, or will he shy away from it like Sandy?

As I was saying, usually only good memories and thoughts surface when I nap with my son. Today, though, things were a bit different.

Justin fell asleep on the couch in the living room while watching Nemo reunite with his dad for the three-millionth time (this week), and I had to carry him to his bed. For some reason - and God only knows where these thoughts come from - carrying my son today brought back a memory of the one and only time I had to carry my father.

Dad was sick. Although he was one of the first people in his crowd to take the Surgeon General seriously and give up smoking his Pall Malls pretty early on in his life, my dad's lungs wound up killing him anyway. He contracted asbestosis from work, which led to the emphysema that left me without a father too early. Way too goddamned early.

I didn't realize it at the time, but I was taking him to the doctor for his final visit. There were no parking spaces close-up and dad couldn't make it to the door on foot; his breath had grown too short by this time to manage more than a few steps. There were no wheelchairs around, so I lifted him out of the car and carried him the 25 or so feet to the entrance where a nurse finally turned up with a chair.

25 feet. Not a very long distance, but I know it felt like a million miles in the mind of a proud man like my father, a man who never needed or wanted to be carried anywhere. And it was more than enough distance for me to realize that there was almost nothing left of my father. He had never been a big man, but he was always scary-strong and tougher than most guys twice his size. Yep, my dad actually coulda whipped your dad. But as I carried him to his doctor's door on that day, I could feel everything that he was and had been was emptying out of him somehow. But he didn't let it go without a fight, he was determined to live his life right up to the end.

This happened close to the same time as that final doctor's visit.

It was a stinking hot August day when I was opening for yet another Nashville star-of-the-moment at yet another dusty county fair. It was a tough slog for even the fittest over the rutted path that led to the stage in the middle of the cow pasture. I looked out during my set and there in the middle of the bared beer-bellies and sweaty halter-tops, was my old man. He had somehow managed, with his electric wheelchair and portable oxygen tank, to get right into the middle of it all. He probably used up his energy for the entire week for the chance to watch me sing five songs.

I think the moment I knew I was going to lose him was the afternoon I came back from Nashville with a video of a performance I had just done at the Bluebird. He was resting in his bed, and I looked in and said, "Hey dad, wanna check out how we stunk up the place in Nashvegas."

He barely opened his eyes, "Maybe later son, maybe later."

Dad died that night. He never saw the video. And I haven't looked at it since.

I am a different kind of father than my dad was. We never said, "I love you" to each other. Even sitting by his bed as he lay dying, I couldn't say the words. It just seemed unnecessary to say out loud what we both already knew. His presence at a thousand Little League games, the countless hours he spent busting his knuckles keeping my cars running, and all of the times he bailed me out of yet another of my seemingly endless jams had already told me everything I needed to know.

Me, I tell my kids I love them about a hundred times a day, not because I am a better father than my dad was - if I wind up being half as good, I'll call that a life well spent - but times have changed and I guess those kinds of things come a little easier these days.

I am sure my dad weighed more on that sad day I carried him to his doctor than Justin does now, but when I carried my son to his bed this afternoon, he seemed heavier, more solid, more 'there' somehow. It is as if he is filling up with the same life force that was emptying out of my dad on that sad day.

I like to take naps with my son. I love my son. And I loved my father. And I have now lived long enough to have carried them both.

I recommend one of those things very highly. And I pray with all of my might that my boy never has to do the other.

Camped Out

A lot of movies feature a clichéd scene of a happy family planning their summer vacation. The dad sits at the kitchen table, which is covered with maps and colorful brochures from amusement parks, mountain resorts and a plethora of historic locations. Mom, dad, Tad Jr. and Miffy and Muffy (the twins) cluster together and consider each destination carefully until a family consensus is reached - and off they go!

As a child, I was always a bit confused by that scene.

Throughout my boyhood, the Weaver clan, rakish thousandaires that we were, did one thing and one thing only on vacation. We went camping. No brochures, no maps, no discussion. And we always camped at the same place. Year after year when the end of July, first of August rolled around, dad would load up the ancient Falcon station wagon and we would head for that glamorous Riviera of the East…

Eagle's Nest Camping Ground in Ocean City, MD. (Ok, technically Berlin, Maryland, but that is just weird)

Yep, we went downy oshin, hon. If you cannot read the previous sentence, you obviously ain't from Maryland…

…hon…

The old Ford would groan in protest as we headed up Ritchie Highway towards Route 50. Slammed to the gills with food, a tent, food, our bedclothes (nothing as fancy as sleeping bags for the Weaver clan) kids, food, assorted dogs and perhaps a neighbor kid or two, the old car often displayed its displeasure by breaking down at interesting and always inopportune times; i.e., miles from anything that resembled a restroom. We peed outside a lot in those days. (Oh, yeah, like you've never done it.)

 I developed a lot of my negotiating skills by haggling with my sisters over who was going to have to sit over the hump in the floor (remember the hump?) in the backseat.

Truly, the ride was part of the fun. We would sing, fight, sleep, eat and generally work overtime at annoying my dad. Of course, he had a trick or two up his sleeve. Both of my parents smoked in those days, so one never knew when a cigarette butt flicked out would make its way into an open window in the back (air conditioning, are you serious?) and find its way into the bedclothes, adding to the fun and mayhem.

I often tell my kids with their bike helmets and knee pads that they would not have survived any random five minutes of my childhood.

But I digress -

The camping spaces at Eagle's Nest resembled nothing so much as they did a carport circa 1962; a concrete slab with a plastic roof, dubious electrical sockets hanging from a rusty metal pole and a leaky spigot supplying all we could drink of salty, warm, brackish lower Eastern Shore water.

The slab was meant to park the car on, so we pitched our tent behind it, next to a drainage ditch. This was actually a much better location to experience the demented, winged, flying fiends that are Ocean City mosquitoes. I swear I used to lie awake at night, listening to them laugh their evil little mosquito laughs as they tore through the impotent mosquito netting with their bare proboscises. We awoke every morning, excited about the coming day, but oddly tired. I realize now it was due to our nightly, albeit involuntary, blood donations.

And speaking of comfort, you will recall that I said that this yearly excursion took place at the end of July, first of August, which is, of course, the perfect time of year to enjoy the biblical humidity that is a seaside-in-Maryland hallmark. Imagine hanging out a wet bathing suit at ten in the morning and checking on it at five in the afternoon, only to find it twice as wet as it was when you hung it up. Actually, the humidity could be looked at as a plus; one could get in a morning swim while walking the dog.

Truth be told, my sisters and I loved that yearly trip across the Bay Bridge. There was a rush of excitement when mom would start frying chicken and making deviled eggs and iced tea the night before. Dad would hose out the red, rusty old cooler, fill it with ice and load in the food. He also packed in the chicken necks we used for crab bait and a few cartons of night crawlers as well. Yep. Right in the same cooler. Hey, nobody died, and we few laughs when scavenging late night family members mistook the worm cartons for leftover Chinese food.

Like my parents were ever going to actually buy food while we were camping. During the week we were there, we ate what came down in the cooler; the chicken and devilled eggs, hot dogs, burgers, cereal and milk. It got pretty gamey and soggy after about five days, but my dad was a firm practitioner of the "if they get hungry enough, they'll eat it" school of nutrition.

If we wanted crabs or fish, you can bet your nether regions that nobody was paying a hundred bucks a bushel, so you had better hope that somebody caught some. We usually did. We fished and crabbed at Eagle's Nest and went to the beach by taking a rowboat across the bay to Assateague Island.

We saw the Ocean City boardwalk exactly twice each trip, one day to go to the beach and eat Thrasher's French fries and one night to hit the arcades, ride some rides and eat Thrasher's French fries. (I believe that research will someday reveal that there is a powerful narcotic in Thrasher's fries. Even my semi-vegetarian-health-food-nut wife craves them.)

Looking back through the haze of those Maryland summer afternoons, I remember those trips as some of the best times of my life. We laughed, swam, sang songs, played guitars, swatted mosquitoes, suffered epic sun burns and sea nettle attacks, fell in and out of summer romances (which also sting, by the way). In short, we lived.

There were no breakfast buffets or hotel rooms, just mom burning some eggs and bacon over a Coleman stove while dad walked us over to the bathhouse for our morning wash up. We would disappear right after breakfast, turn up at lunch time for a quick leftover Esskay hotdog and ketchup on Blue Ribbon bread sandwich and take off again until the full moon rose up over the ocean.

I always wondered what my mom and dad did in that stuffy old tent all day while we were gone. Now that I have kids of my own, I think I can guess.

My wife and I have been needing some quality time. Time to load up the minivan…

Pap's Shotgun

Everybody called my grandfather Pap. He was a typical Maryland man of a certain age. He farmed, hunted, fished, crabbed, smoked, cussed...

Pap was what they called a 'man's man' in those days. And like all men's men, he was a hunter.

Me, I wasn't much of a hunter. For various reasons, not the least of which being that a lot of hunting is done in the winter and I hate cold weather, the whole thing just didn't take with me. By the time I was in my teens I had given up any pretense of even faking it.

The fact that I did not hunt in no way meant that I wanted to miss the annual day-after-Thanksgiving deer hunting trip to Maryland's Eastern Shore. Sleeping crammed in a tiny, ancient metal camper with Pap, my dad and his brothers gave me a chance to see these men away from wives, sisters, daughters and my Grandma. I saw a flash of the wild boys these rough hewn men used to be.

I was supposed to cook to earn my keep, until I nearly burned down the trailer trying to make hamburgers. After that, it was decided that maybe I should just "take care of Pap".

The problem with that plan was that Pap didn't want any goddamn part of being taken care of.

Deer hunting was probably the safest thing for Pap and I to do together when I was a teenager. No one talks much when while they're hunting and Pap and I had reached a point where we didn't have much to say to each other. As my hair got longer and my clothes got weirder, he basically viewed me as an alien creature not part of his world.

I didn't hunt, I hated the farm, I only worked on cars when I absolutely had to, I played the guitar in a rock and roll band and generally seemed to be on the opposite side of whatever he stood for. He didn't have much use for me and had no problem letting me know it.

Just a week before one hunting trip, I was walking home from school in the pouring November rain when I saw Pap coming up the road in his old Chevy truck and tried to wave him down.

He drove right by me.

When I finally got to the house, soaked to the skin and freezing, I asked,

"Hey Pap, didn't you see me?"

"I saw you just fine."

"Well, why did't you stop? It's pouring out there."

"I told you last week to get a goddamn haircut. You ain't got one yet. I can't have somethin' that looks like you in my truck. I gotta live in this neighbourhood."

We didn't have much to talk about, Pap and me.

As the years wore on, I started to have to give Pap a boost to get him up into his tree stand. The years, miles and Camels were riding him down. The year finally came when it was clear that he wasn't going to be able to get up into his stand, or even walk too far into the woods at all.

I walked with him to the edge of a winter cornfield, where we sat in a shallow trench that had been turned up by tractor tires and plows. It was freezing and Pap was old.

He wrapped himself up in some blankets and a sleeping bag. If a deer had actually wandered by, it would have had to wait patiently for its chance to become venison while Pap sat up, unwrapped himself, grabbed his old shotgun and finally fired off a shot.

I guess maybe he realised that there was little chance that he was going to bag his limit, because, wonder of wonders, Pap actually spoke to me.

"Heard you playing that banjer of yours with them boys up the hill t'other night."

I didn't play the banjo then or now. It was a Fender Mustang and I was playing a Grand Funk Railroad song with a very loud - and very lousy - rock trio.

"Sorry Pap. Was it too loud? Couldn't you hear the ballgame?"

"Nah. That music you play ain't to my taste for sure, but it sounded like you might know what you're doin'."

I have had a few successes in my life, but I don't remember ever having a greater sense of accomplishment than I did at that moment on that frigid morning sitting with my grandfather in that nameless Eastern Shore cornfield.

That was November. Pap was dead by Christmas. I was his oldest grandson, so his ancient but perfectly kept old shotgun came to me.

A lot of deer seasons have come and gone since my grandma handed me that old 12 gauge, and I haven't shot it once. I hate it when things that once had a purpose start to gather dust or wind up as decorations on the wall of some lousy Americana-themed chain restaurant. Everything and everyone should be allowed to work as long as they can and then retire with dignity and not become some sort of bullshit sideshow.

When my mother gently suggested that one of my cousins that hunts would love to have my grandfather's shotgun, well, it just felt right. I knew he would clean it, oil it up, shoot it and give it back the purpose it was made for.

I think Pap would be pleased. He might even say, "Boy, you just might know what you're doin'."

It occurs to me that I have now lived more of my life away from the Chesapeake Bay than I have lived close to it. No matter. I was born, and I remain, a Chesapeake son of the 'Chesapeake Sun'.

Chesapeake Sun

Sometimes I say I come from California,
a Nashville address was good for my career.
It never feels quite real to me, to say I come from Tennessee,
truth be told, I grew up right around here.

I know the smell of the salt water marshes,
the rhythm of a river in the rain.
August when it's too damn hot,
Blue crabs steamin' in a pot,
That Old Bay she's runnin' through my veins.

Now the years and miles roll out behind me,
no matter how far I try to run.
In my dreams, I find my place
I wake up with it on my face,
the sweet kiss of a Chesapeake Sun.

Snow geese above a frozen cornfield,
up in the morning running a trot line.
When your waiting at your heaven's gate,
tell the good Lord he'll have to wait,
I want another season here in mine

Now the years and miles roll out behind me,
no matter how far I try to run.
In my dreams, I find my place
I wake up with it on my face,
the sweet kiss of a Chesapeake Sun.

Yeah, the years and miles roll out behind me,

no matter how far I try to run.
In all my dreams, I find my place
I wake up with it on my face,
the sweet kiss of a Chesapeake Sun.

I am a Chesapeake Son.

All of the songs from A Father's Heart are available at http://weaverwrites. com/songs_from_a_fathers_heart

Momma's Boy

I have written reams and reams worth of copy about my dad, but mentions of my mom have been few and far between. I guess some things are just harder - closer to the bone, maybe.

Mothers and sons - the relationship that keeps therapists the world over in sail boats and Ferraris.

Irish American/Southern mothers and sons - enough drama to keep Dr. Phil busy enough that he will never have to write another book about weight loss.

My mother endured a childhood of such soul-crushing poverty that getting even the cliched piece of fruit in a Christmas stocking would have been a slice of heaven. Too many kids and too little money combined with an alcoholic, abusive father to create a nightmare that would have broken most people. I would never betray my mother's trust by cataloging the horrors that were her every day as a child, and, in truth, you don't want to know.

In attempts to avoid the monster she was married to, my grandmother and the little girl that would grow into my mom would window shop on the streets of Baltimore for hours on end. Mom told us that her mother would always say, "One day honey, when we get rich, I'll buy you that baby doll. And a new dress."

I never got to know my grandmother. She was murdered by her husband when my mother was still just a child, so she never got the chance to buy my mother a baby doll. Or a dress.

My mother has collected dolls for her entire adult life. Perhaps she is still trying to find that one that she ached for in that dirty Baltimore store front window.

As I said, I never knew my grandmother, but I suspect I would have liked her.
My mom loves to tell a story about the day her family moved from West Virginia to a row house in Baltimore. Upon hearing her mountain accent, the kid next door started taunting my mom and calling her a "hillbilly".

My grandmother sent mom back outside with a message to the punk next door,
"You tell him that there's only two kinds of people that lives in Maryland, Nellie.
One's a hillbilly and the other's a son-of-a-bitch, and we know which one we are."

Against all odds, mom grew into a happy woman with a sparkling smile and a boisterous laugh. Our's was the house where neighbourhood kids felt welcome enough to rummage through the refrigerator without asking. They knew Miss Nellie would not be mad if they had a baloney (and yes, I spell it baloney…the way I say it. I don't know that I have ever eaten bologna) sandwich. She'd be more pissed because they felt like they had to ask.

Miss Nellie has never met a stranger. She is the slightly wacky lady in the Baltimore Raven's sweatshirt that just starts talking to you while you are in line at the bank or supermarket. Get her started, brother, and my mom can talk the bark off a pine tree.

And yeah, she passed that bit of DNA on to her son.

Her tear ducts are located directly on the surface of her face. She cries at school plays, Brownie fly-ups, six grade graduations, when the dog gets a haircut…

When I hit my first Little League home run, she ran the bases with me. She may have actually crossed home plate before I did.

She made our lunches, walked us to the bus stop and sang to us - whether we wanted her to our not. My mom has at best a very casual relationship with the actual lyrics to most songs, but what she doesn't know, she makes up. I have passed on her fractured versions of many a lullaby to my kids.

She was there for us, every day, with a love so unconditional that it can be pretty tough to live up to.

In one of the cruelest blows that has ever been visited, the universe decided to take my sister from her before she was even out of her teens. How fate can steal a child from a woman that has dedicated her life to being a mother - especially after what she herself endured as a child - is a question I will never be able to answer.

As her only son, I have been the object of some of my mom's most aggressive spoiling. As such, I admit to being pretty damn rotten as a kid.

When I started getting the dreaded 'momma's boy' tag as a teenager, I probably tried to cut the apron strings with a bit more force than was necessary. It hurt her, and I'm an ass for doing it.

So much of who I am - the music, the love of language and spinning a good yarn, it all comes from her.

Like a good mother should, she makes me crazy. She tells the same damn stories, over and over, talking for hours about people she swears that I know but I have never met. When she tells me about a TV show she watched, it is not a synopsis. It is real time rendering, complete with all of the dialogue and sound effects intact.

The image of my mom that always pops into my head is one from a lot of years ago, way before cordless phones.

Every morning of my grade school life, there's Nellie, phone cricked between her shoulder and her ear, talking to her sister on the phone with an L&M cigarette hanging from her lips, WCAO on the kitchen radio, making breakfast and school lunches at the same time, all the while wrapping a 25 foot phone cord around chairs, kids, dogs or anything else sleepy or foolish enough to get in her way.

The lunches were always the same: Baloney on Blue Ribbon white bread with Hellman's Real Mayonnaise, a small bag of Utz potato chips and a Tastykake Butterscotch Krimpet. Not a scrap of vitamins or minerals, or even real food, anywhere, and yet, somehow, I survived.

One of the reasons I was reluctant to start this story is that I knew I'd have a hard time finding a way to end it.

I live far away form my mother now, and I miss her. Some days all I want to do, is sit at her table with a baloney sandwich - and I haven't eaten baloney in about 30 years - and listen to her tell me one of her endless stories. Sure, I know how it would end - if it actually had an end - but the secret is in the telling…and in the storyteller.

By the way, if, after reading all of this, you feel the urge to call me a momma's boy, go right ahead. I'll consider it a compliment.

Old Toy Trains

'Old Toy Trains' is the title a great old Roger Miller song. Toy trains are always the first thing that pop into my head when Christmas is closing in.

My dad made sure that we had a Christmas garden every year. It was not some elaborate vanity project with flowing waterfalls and self-propelled people, though.

Our Christmas village was a 4x6 piece of plywood that dad nailed to some two-by-sixes. He painted the whole thing green, drilled some holes big enough to stick big, screw-in Christmas lights through - to light the houses, of course - used some left-over black stove paint to make a few roads and finally screwed an oval of model train tracks around the perimeter. It sat dormant and dusty in our basement all year until December rolled around and it was time to hit the rust on the tracks with some steel wool, add some plastics houses along with plastic people, cars, trucks and animals from various play sets, put an old mirror in the middle to become a frozen lake, hit the whole mess with some canned snow and…

Magic.

My sisters set up the houses and stuff, but the trains…the trains were mine.

Lionel trains. Big trains. I never learned the name of all the gauges, just that HO was puny, and these were the big ones.

Some of them my dad had carried with him from his childhood. He polished and cherished them the way one does when they came up hard and learned the value of things.

The crisp, dusty, almost dangerous smell of electricity frying ozone when he plugged in the big transformer and hooked up the wires to the track is a much an olfactory memory of Christmas to me as are the scent of pine, tangerines and roast turkey.

Dad would set the speed on the transformer so that the locomotive and all of the freight cars would make it smoothly around the oval. Behind the engine and the coal car came a Baby Ruth car, a B&O Railroad car, an ESSO (not Exxon) tanker car, a lumber car, a few others and, of course, the caboose. They rumbled majestically around the track, past the tranquil village where the big old-fashioned Christmas lights were warping and melting the plastic houses, were the mismatched figurines were creating scale issues that resulted in sheep being bigger than the houses and ducks on the mirror pond the same size as the Buicks on the street next door, where the sticky fake snow was getting dusty and grey.

God…it was beautiful…

I love trains and have been to any number of elaborate holiday displays over the years and have yet to see one as cool as my dad's knotty, peeling plywood township.

Please, don't get me started on theme Christmas trees and gardens where everything matches and everything is planned to bland perfection.

Bah, humbug!

I, of course, ran many tests to see how fast I could get the trains to go before they jumped the track - usually behind the the tree. I staged spectacular train wrecks involving toy cars and the giant mutant farm animals.

The old man was not thrilled.

This was a very delicately balanced enterprise. Our Christmas tree stand was a Maxwell House coffee can covered in wrapping paper and filled with sand. It was always a safe bet that before the whole beautiful mess came down after New Year's that the tree would have to be wired to the nail that hung year-round in the corner and the garden would become a mine field of glass shards from fallen ornaments.

I would love to tell you that I carried the train garden traditional on with my own kids, but I didn't. I think the whole thing was so hard-wired in my heart to my dad, that it seemed wrong somehow that it went on without him.

Everyone has their Christmas moments. The ones that bring that joy mixed with wistfulness tear; watching 'It's a Wonderful Life', hanging up that ornament from someone who has gone, finding an old card…

For me, when I hear Roger Miller strumming his nylon string and he starts to sing,

"Old toy trains, little toy tracks, little boy toys, comin' from a sack…"

Well, I'm gonna need a moment…

I just noticed that there are a couple of Christmas stories here. I'm an agnostic, not-too-connected-with-organised anything kinda guy, but the home and family parts of the holidays have always meant a lot to me. 'Christmas in Copenhagen, 1996' is the exact opposite of your average Hallmark Christmas movie. It is, in fact, perhaps the most depressing holiday song ever.

I'm kind of proud of that.

Christmas in Copenhagen

Christmastime, Copenhagen, 1996.
The weather's been shit for weeks, everybody's sick.
Rain freezin' on the window, but this car is way too hot.
This train sounds like pneumonia, wheezin' from stop to stop.
To another station up ahead, with another name I can't pronounce
I just count the times we stop so I know just when to get out,
into a freezin' rain that steals my heart and chills me to the bone,
I woulda stopped to call you, but I can't figure out the phones

Tonight I wish this train rain all the way to Texas,
and made a stop in Tennessee.
On a downtown station where a little green-eyed girl is,
waitin' on the platform just for me.
'til it steals your heart, you'll never know just what cold is,
Tonight I wish this train rain all the way to Texas.

Nørreport to Nyhavn, it's 22 city blocks,
I can't afford a taxi, so I guess I'll have to walk.
Every door holds a troubadour, his case open at his feet,
singin' over top the steam grates, tryin' to catch a little heat
Fingers cut out of his gloves, just so he can play,
'til it gets so goddamn cold it don't matter anyway
"Knockin' on Heaven's Door" in an accent I don't know,
"Take Me Home, Country Roads", I got 16 blocks to go.

Tonight I wish this train rain all the way to Texas,

and made a stop in Tennessee.
On a downtown station where a little green-eyed girl is,
waitin' on the platform just for me.
'til it steals your heart, you'll never know just what cold is,
Tonight I wish this train rain all the way to Texas.

One last round of Christmas cheer, time to catch the
midnight train,
22 city blocks back uptown through the snow and freezin'
rain.
I saw a lady on the smoking car in her bright red Christmas
dress,
her head slumped against the window, she had a long night
too, I guess
I recall that I first saw her when we both were comin' in,
before the promise of the season had let us down again.
When she was gettin' dress tonight, she never dreamed she
would explain,
that the only man who brought her home was some
stranger on the train.

Tonight I wish this train rain all the way to Texas,
and made a stop in Tennessee.
On a downtown station where a little green-eyed girl is,
waitin' on the platform just for me.
'til it steals your heart, you'll never know just what cold is,
Tonight I wish this train rain all the way to Texas.

(c) 2016 Ray Weaver

All of the songs from A Father's Heart are available at
http://weaverwrites.
com/songs_from_a_fathers_heart

Danish for Beginners

No matter how long we have been living here, when a bunch of expats meet up in a pub anywhere in Denmark we assiduously avoid speaking Danish at every opportunity. Most of us can mumble a few phrases, at various levels of competence, but it really does make your head hurt after a while.

Let's face it. Danish is simply unpronounceable to anyone not born in Denmark. I think there is a chemical reaction that happens when leverpostej is smeared on rugbrød that renders a Danish child's tongue able to say the words.

Extra letters. Why? No, really. Why? So you have a written version of something that sounds like you are choking on a pork rind?

And of course, no matter how many times our Danish friends and significant others rail at us that we should "Snak dansk for helvede!" ("Speak Danish, goddammit!") as soon as we do, they switch to English.

Their delicate ears are simply not accustomed to hearing their musical, mellifluous language spoken with an ugly coarse, foreign accent. Heaven forfend!

But, there is fun to be had whilst wading through Danskland.

As a musician, I learned early on not to ask a Danish guitarist if I could borrow his pi(c)k. My elderly, teetotaling mother nearly required smelling salts and a whisky after my Danish wife told her she was very pleased that I was such a great kok in the kitchen. And my microwave calls me a slut every time my Thai box has finished heating properly.

There is not one English-speaking tourist that ever visited the Little Mermaid that has not snapped a photo of at least one 'Turist fart' sign. I know I have.

If you are not sure why any of the above are funny, it's your Danish assignment this week to find out why.

One of the things any expat learns to love about Danish is its literalness. How can you not love a language in which the word for gums literally translates as 'tooth meat', a vacuum cleaner is a 'dust sucker', a refrigerator is a 'cold closet' and a lawn mower is, wait for it, a 'grass hitting machine'.

It's simply brilliant!

Although Danes are loathe to hear expats butcher their language, they are quite proud of their ability to speak English, and regale us with it at every opportunity. Unfortunately, much of their knowledge comes from teachers. I was bemused - and, ok, a little pissed off - the first time I had a parent/teacher conference with my son's English teacher and he told me, right up front, "I don't speak English."

Many Danes get much of their English from films and there is no filter on Danish TV as to who is watching what when. "Natural Born Killers' might be the lead-in for

'Frozen' at pretty much any time regular Danish channels. Bare breasts and profanity abound in what would be considered family viewing hours in most of the English speaking world.

One of my first encounters with Danes speaking English was in the company of a father and his two picture-perfect, blonde-haired, blue-eyed young children on a windswept beach on the Danish island of Bornholm.

Twenty years ago, Yanks on Bornholm were a bit of a novelty, so the dad was excited to introduce me to the kids,

"This is Ray. He comes from America. He speaks English. Say something to him in English."

I could see the beautiful blue-eyed boy struggling, desperately seeking to impress me with a suitable English phrase.

"Fuck you!" he squeaked happily.

"You fucking motherfucker!" his sister joyfully exclaimed.

Their dad beamed.

Some Closing Words for my Children

Walk outside.

Enjoy the sun.

Experience the cold.

Never mind the rain.

The wood of the finest guitar was once a tree that drew its life from the elements as it grew.

It gathered the stories of the animals that passed its way, collected the secrets of the forest and sun and sky, and held them deep inside until a master craftsman shaped the wood into music and allowed those stories and secrets to burst forth in songs.

Your own music is waiting inside of you.

Nurture it.

Help it grow.

Walk outside.

I like beginnings and endings. I like bookends. We came in with a bit of music, and so let's close with one last song. 'At the End of the Day' is my 9/11 song. Some hear it as a song about a woman. Some hear it as a hymn. I'm good with either interpretation. When the world seemed at its darkest, at the end of that sad, sad day I knew where I had to go. Home.

At the End of the Day

At the End of the Day, when even my soul is weary.
At the end of the Day, when I'm sure even God can't hear
me.
When dreams fail and vision falters, the burden is too
much to bear.
At the End of the Day, I know you'll be there.

At the End of the Day, when sunlight fails the sky.
At the End of the Day, when the news is too sad to cry.
When my nets have all come up empty, and I wonder why
I even care.
At the End of the Day, I know you'll be there.

Sometimes it's all that I can do, to make my way home to
you.

At the End of the Day, when there's only you and me.
At the End of the Day, your touch will set me free.
With the world finally locked outside, you answer me like
a prayer
At the End of the Day, I know you'll be there,
At the End of the Day, I know you'll be there.
(c) 2016 Ray Weaver/Morten Wittrock

All of the songs from A Father's Heart are available at
http://weaverwrites.
com/songs_from_a_fathers_heart

Credits:

The music included in this book stretches back nearly 40 years. It is impossible for me to remember everyone that played on every song, so I'll give a few shout outs with apologies to those I may forget. Get in touch, and I'll include your name next time around.

People who have made immeasurable contributions to the songs here include:

Morten Wittrock, Chip Davis, Billy Davis, Lars Krarup, Mike Mumford, Al Perkins, Mikkel Risum, Ken Weaver, Mike Vinson, Jacob Rathje, Valerie Vigoda, Martin Seidelin … and more …

Cover art: Justin Raymond Weaver

Made in the USA
Columbia, SC
23 November 2018